Flowers For Mama

Candia Cumberbatch-Lucenius

Publisher: Grace Independent Media Group

ISBN: :10: 0692695397
ISBN-13: 978-0692695395

DEDICATION

Lovingly dedicated to Mary M. Cumberbatch.

CONTENTS

ACKNOWLEDGMENTS

To God be the glory, great things He has done. The words of this song says what I want to say first and foremost. It is only by the grace of God this book has become a reality.

Next I want to acknowledge all the wonderful people in my life for their love, support and contribution

My husband of 20 years (at this writing)

> ***Jon Scott Lucenius.*** You have always been so supportive and encouraging; you remember to tell me you love me every day – many times a day. That love and encouragement from God's Word has helped me through many a dark day of loss and sadness in our family.

My son

> ***Swanson Avelino Candius Charles*** – my son who I love and admire, and proud of his accomplishments in his career in sales; and his daughter *Jemini Jade Lagueux* – a beautiful, smart, intelligent young lady – so proud of you and love

you lots.

My daughter

Makeeva Andrewna Candacey Charles – who I love for her strength to keep learning as a mother and phlebotomist; and her children *Avelino Ralph Isaac, and Saiah Ivy Lilliana* – who inspire me to keep growing and learning as a mother. Lots of love.

My sisters

Evarist Charlotte Nova Cumberbatch-Pittman, (my oldest sister) – who I love for her consistent love for her family - her children and grandchildren:

Kima Golda Fern Cumberbatch-Chitolie and her son *Kimson Max Chitolie.* "I love and respect her for her love for God and His Word, her committed moral compass and strength to overcome one day at a time in the face of adversity."

Tamarana Hyacinth Nina and her children *Terrinika Clarke, Morgan Cumberbatch. Marlan Biscette.*

Krista Naomi Janelle and her children *Abigail*

Steele, Priscilla Steele, Joshua Steele Jr, and Naomi Steele.

Love and blessings

Karan Lillian Mary (followed in Mama's footsteps – teacher/educator/ counsellor/ mentor) – I love you for your strength to overcome and keep going by God's grace. Such a blessing to me and so many others. Thanks for being my prayer partner, and counsellor as well as Natural Health Coach; and her children

Dr. Marvourneen Kimranee Dolor, Tamilia Marie Dolor (daughters) and *Francois Casabianca*. I love and am so proud of each of you – smart, intelligent and so supportive of their mother and each other.

Kathleen Lois (Registered Nurse) – I love you for being so strong and resilient – the fun nest sister; and her children *Carlene Shanda Lee Marie* (daughter) and her son *Ayodele* – I love & admire her strength to get up and dust herself off and keep going.

Benson Lennon and *David Elijah* (sons)

Love you all.

My brothers:

> ***Abraham Ralph Cumberbatch*** (deceased) – still love and miss him every day
> ***Isaac Wayne Cumberbatch*** – followed in Mama's footsteps – a teacher/educator – will always love you.

Every one of them – some a lot more than others have been an inspiration to me leading up to writing this book.

My many extended family members and special friends and their families who contributed and allowed me to include a special tribute to their mothers.

God's blessings to each and every one of you. I will try to mention all by name if it's possible.

Prologue

When I first thought about writing a tribute to my mother, in my head it was going to be a short story. After listening to so many of my friends and family members relay stories of their mothers, God laid it on my heart to allow others to contribute to this endeavor and have the opportunity to share their tributes to their mothers as well.

This is a compilation of many stories, poems and thoughts of what as I encouraged them to do is write anything you would say to your mother or about her, whether she is still here with us or not.

This has been and continues to be a very emotional journey for me. As like many others might say, the relationship I have with my mother has not always been a smooth one. The one constant though is I know she loves me, she wants the best for me and she wants to make sure I am born again and living a life that will bring glory to our Heavenly Father God and His Son Jesus Christ. So, like my father used to say "age brings reason." As I got older it dawned on me that although not perfect she did the absolute best with what she knew. My mother's love for her children was not always vocalized, but it showed in all she did for us.

"Give me my flowers while I am alive, because I cannot enjoy them when I'm gone." That is a phrase I heard my mother use many times over the years, and although I'm not sure where it originated that's what inspired the title for my book. For years I looked at it as literal flowers. I started making sure my mother had flowers every birthday, Mother's Day and Christmas Day. Although I still do that, I've long since realized (my 'AHA' moment) that the "flowers" here could mean, love, attention, gifts, time, a surprise birthday party, a spa day, a trip overseas to visit family, a listening ear – whatever is needed at the time.

~ A Phenomenal Woman ~

Mrs. Mary M. Cumberbatch is a phenomenal woman. She's Mama or Ma to all - her children, grandchildren, great grandchildren and many of our friends. Mrs. Cumberbatch or "Miss" to her past students (she was an Elementary School teacher for about 30 or more years), to her friends she's Ma Cumby or Ma Cumber or sister Cumby and to others in her family she is Hillis or Aunty Hillis. Whatever you call her, she is a legend, loved and respected by all who have had the pleasure of knowing her.

We honored Mama at a special surprise birthday celebration when she turned 80 years old on April 25th 2014 – 80 years of tears, love, and laughter. The look on her face at that special surprise was priceless – she knew we were planning something she had no idea how glamorous it would turn out to be.

Mama with my sisters and brothers at her 80th Birthday

Party – we had so much fun celebrating her life and giving her "her flowers" on her special day!

My first special moment with Mama, that I remember, was when I was 5 years old. I don't remember if we were walking or just sitting on the steps as many of us do at home in Fort, St. Lucia, but I remember asking her "Mama, how do I get saved?" She quietly replied "you need to accept Jesus Christ as your Savior" and proceeded to teach me how to say what most Christians for years called "the sinners pray." Over the years I thought about it many times which led to me always asking questions in church and to anyone else who would listen about the Bible, God and Jesus Christ. To this day, I am thankful to my mother's teaching of God's Word to all her children, grandchildren and even some of her great grandchildren. That has been the foundation, the standard for my moral compass in all my decision making in life and for that I owe her a wealth of gratitude.

It was not always easy for Ma raising 6 children – 4 girls and 2 boys, basically by herself. The love story started off great – a nursing student at Victoria Hospital, Castries St. Lucia, falling for the dashing, handsome, "phylozoff" (as Ma sometimes called him) police officer, originally from Barbados. Maybe it was his smile, the jokes he loved to tell, or maybe just the uniform, but before she knew it, Mama was pregnant and married.

As many who knew her growing up, say "Hillis was spoiled, first by her father, who she attributes to first telling her about God, and who she lost as a teenager-devastating her; then by her aunt, Auntee Maltide, who she went to live with when she started high school at the St. Mary's Convent," a prestigious all-girls school, and then by her husband – Daddy – Eustace A. Cumberbatch.

 We are all very familiar with how the love story changes – before long she was no longer being spoiled and pampered – being left alone as he was transferred to different cities as a cop. By then, Mama had 6 children – Wayne was a baby when she first realized (even though she had her suspicions) that Daddy's "transfers" were not truly all about work.

MA.....MAMA......MOTHER......MAMURR.!!

GROWING UP IN VIEUX FORT
THE FOOLISHEST OF THE BUNCH
BLACK, AND UGLY.....SO....CRAZY I SHOULD
BE,........I THOUGHT !

I FOUGHT, I CRIED, I REBELLED AGAINST
THE TEACHINGS, THE WHIPPINGS, THE CHORES
THE LESSONS LEARNED WERE PASSED ON
THRU THE DOORS
TO MY OFFSPRING...ALTHOUGH....YES THEY
WERE CONDENSED

WE TELL OURSELVES "I WON'T BE LIKE THAT
TO MY KIDS
BUT...MAMA KNOWS BEST, CAN'T YOU SEE?
YOU SPARE THE ROD AND SPOIL THE CHILD
SO...TEACH THEM "CORRECTLY" SO THEY HEED

MAMA IS TOUGH, SHE CAN BE QUITE ROUGH
BUT SHE ONLY WANTS, WHATS BEST FOR HER
KIDDOS
DONT POUT OUT YOUR MOUTH AND CHOOPS
LIKE A FOOL
SHES BEEN THERE, AND DONE THAT, SO
LISTEN AND FOLLOW THE RULES

YES....LISTEN AND BEWARE, AS THEY SAY
LAPWEEYEH
IS A POWERFUL THING, PARKAR JWAY
SHES A PRAYING WOMAN, A GODLY WOMAN
IT AINT HARD TO KNOW, IT'S NOT JUST A VISION

*THIS WOMAN, I SPEAK OF IS MY MAMA YOU
KNOW....
BEY LEY LEY......IM THE ONLY REPLICA
OF THE PHYSICAL ASPECT OF HER*

MORE LOVE, MA

**KATHEE
KATHLEEN LOIS CUMBERBATCH
COMPOSED ON 05/07/2016**

~ No More Spoiling or Pampering ~

Life as she knew it was over – no more spoiling or pampering – she had 6 children to raise and feed. So, what did Mama do? Maybe not the next day, but she decided that God would be her sufficiency and relied on him day by day to provide. Mama made a decision that she couldn't or maybe wouldn't go back to nursing school and so started teaching and went to Teachers College to get the education she needed. Her strength and reliance even when it seems the whole world was on her shoulder, was amazing. When life knocked her down, and it seemed like she may not be able to get up, so many times I saw her almost use a spatula to peel herself off the floor/ground, just enough to get on her knees. Once there she opened her heart to God time and time again, ending in just an amazing song of praise and worship. It was then she was able to dust herself off, stand on her feet and keep going.

Mama always encouraged her children to study, do

our homework and work hard.

Another time in my life growing up when I experienced my mother's love for children, and how much she depended on God for His strength and support and her knowing and believing He would answer her was during my sister Karan's illness. Now, I cannot remember how old she was when she was diagnosed with epilepsy, but Karan would have severe epileptic attacks, which would come on at any time day or night. I remember listening to my parents talk about it, and even some leaders of the church discussing the prognosis. The doctors told our parents that due to the severity of the epilepsy, Karen would not survive, and if she did she would be a "vegetable." They even suggested our parents take Karan out of school because of the chances of her getting hurt whenever she had an attack. There were many tears and prayers shed for this beautiful, energetic, otherwise healthy looking girl who no medicine seemed to help.

After one of her many hospitalizations when Karan packed up her little suitcase and left the hospital "AMA" (against medical advice), I much later learned it was called, she was found in a gutter after one of these epileptic attacks and brought home.

Mama called the pastor, and church leaders; I remember Daddy being there as well; I don't remember what the conversation was all about but I do remember someone reading from the Bible – I Timothy (the verse about anointing the head with oil, laying hands and pray for the sick); then them pouring oil on Karan's head – everyone putting their hands on her head while the pastor prayed. There was not a dry eye in the room.

It wasn't long after that (cannot remember how long exactly) that I remember some gradual improvement in Karan – less frequent attacks.

Over the years she has remained on maintenance doses of medications, but has been able to live a full live. Even after missing weeks of school, Karan graduated from High School with distinctions and top of her class. She attended a Bible College for two years in Jamaica, and went on to Teachers College on her return. Karan had a very successful career as a teacher, Principal, and Chief Education Officer, where even today she is well known and highly respected in the Ministry of Education in St. Lucia. She also completed degrees in Education; was married twice and has 3 grown children – very intelligent, successful and accomplished. I attribute God's miraculous healing power on Karan is due to Mama's unrelenting faith and belief that God didn't want her to lose her child and that He was not only able but willing to heal her. (Certainly didn't come from Daddy).

During all this, Mama still had to raise her other 5 children who were still quite young. Her mother, who she hoped would step in and help, lived at the other end of the island and was not much help for the day to day needs of a young mother with a very sick child. At a young age we learned to pray, believe and trust God.

We learned much later that Mama had many suitors who offered to help her with her six children since Mr. Cumberbatch was not pulling his weight. She graciously rejected all those offers, deciding instead to rely on God to provide as well as her "church family," who had a hand in helping us by supplying food, a roof when ours was under repair, discipline when Mama was at work or even just telling her where one of her children was seen – usually where they were not supposed to be :-)

While dealing with all these upheavals in her life, Mama thrived as a teacher – seemed she was a natural born teacher. She always went above and beyond, staying after school and even on weekends to work with a slow child or giving extra help to a promising one who needed that gentle push of encouragement. From her dedicated, hard work have come principals, teachers, nurses and many other professions. To this day, Mama is stopped by a past student or one of their children who have heard stories of this amazing, loving, caring teacher who without her they would be no-where. The hugs, and tears as they remind her of how she nurtured them as one of her own. Thanking her over and over again has brought so much joy to her as well as her children. It fills our hearts with pride to call her Mama.

If that wasn't enough, Mama, tirelessly it seemed, continued to help raise a few of her grandchildren way into her retirement years. You wouldn't believe it, but she tried to help raise a few of her great grands as well, but her body reminded her that she had done enough. So now, she leaves the child raising to the younger generation, but continues to teach all she can about God and His Word to all who would listen. If you do not have at least 30 – 40 minutes to spare, do not call Mama. No matter how many times you say, "This is just a quick call to say..." be prepared for whatever you called about to be turned into a mini sermon by Mama. So still, many – not just the children call her to talk, to share and to pray.

Mama was always an avid reader – another trait passed on to her children and many of her grandchildren. Mama could always be found reading in her "quiet" time – which was not too often. I still burst out in laughter when I remember Mama having to go to the bathroom and looking for a book, magazine or Readers Digest to take with her. Since that was the longest quiet time she probably would have, Mama would "hold it in" until she found the right reading material before she headed to the bathroom. If at times she knew she wouldn't make it in time, she ran in and called to one of us to bring it to her. "Get my Bible/Readers Digest/magazine off the bookshelf, and bring it to me please." We laughed as we echoed the same thing each time. "Mama go on; what if you don't get there in time!!" "Out of the way" she would say as she ran in – in the nick of time.

Mama

Everyone, it seems calls her Mama
She graciously accepts it and responds.
I never once heard her say, "I'm not your mother"
She quietly smiles and doesn't bother.

Starting her career in nursing as a teenager, then
Fell in love, got married and started a family
Years later she re-invented herself as a teacher
Still answering her calling to care for and nurture

Sometimes tough and foreboding on the outside,
In her role as teacher, leader and guidance counsellor.
And as Mama, she kept on teaching about God and life
Trying to keep everyone on the straight and narrow.

She stayed on her knees, going to God for everything.
"I learned about God from my father," she says with
pride.
"I can still recall some of those Bible stories he told us"

The sadness in her eyes still lingering after all these years.

So as I give God thanks for my Godly Mama,
I have to be thankful for her father as well
We never knew him, he died when she was a teenager
But he helped shape her life into the God fearing Mama
we know.

Candia Cumberbatch-Lucenius
March 26th, 2016

~ *Friends Honoring Their Mothers* ~

As I mentioned at the beginning this book is not just about Mama. It's about the millions of mother's some still here and some who have passed on, who may or may not have been recognized for their hard work, their tireless devotion. This is to all or as many as would like to say something to or about their mother and give her the flowers she deserves even if she is no longer here to enjoy them. It's a tribute collection to share with the world.

"She knows what I'm like, and loves me anyway. I love you Mama!"

Marvourneen Kimranee Dolor, PhD (granddaughter)

March 22nd, 2016

"Mothers are the reason we are alive and we grow up strong. Thanks to Mama for my mom."

Swanson A. C. Charles.

April 16th, 2016

~ Carol's Reflection ~

Carol strong in faith, beauty and grace,

Warmth and kindness in her face.

An angel sent from above,

With a heart so full of love.

She has glamour, she has style,

She is a woman full of pride.

A rainbow to brighten your darkest day,

She is the light that shines our way.

Walking the path of truth and love,

She has the touch, gentle as a dove.

Embraces the true essence of motherhood.

In everyone, she sees the good.

She is the rock we all lean on,

From setting sun to early dawn.

Our strength in times when we feel weak,

For nurturing and guidance it's her we seek.

Her faith in God is tried and true,

Persevere and never give up is what you do.

Creative in so many ways,

Knows hard work and determination always pays.

Pearls of wisdom and diamonds glowing,

Our love for her always showing.

Carol, strong in faith and beauty and grace,

The light of your life shines in your face.

For all that you are and all you have been,

You are our true Caribbean Queen,

by Esther Charles

April 25th, 2009

~ *Proverbs 22:6* ~

Train up a child in the way he should go: and when he is old, he will not depart from it.

My mother, as a single parent, raised four children. We had everything we needed. She is my inspiration because I saw her constantly go to God in prayer and believing and God always came through.

She gave us the foundation upon which to build our lives and inspired me to want to know more about our Heavenly Father. This led me to The Way ministry for which I am so thankful for teaching me Biblical research keys and making available God's rightly divided Word enabling me and my family to claim an abundance of His promises.

By Carolyn Pryor

March 23rd, 2016

~ My Mom ~

The meaning of mom can be bitter sweet...a stern disciplinarian and yet a caring friend. A rule maker and thankfully, a rule breaker. My journey with Mom has been not only bitter sweet for these reasons, but also because there were times in our youth I couldn't understand some of the choices she made. Living through some disappointments I grew to admire her quiet strength. The more spiritually mature I become, the more I appreciate the mother I was blessed to have. Through the years, I am grateful that God has opened my eyes to this fact.

I want my mom to know that she taught me a lot about endurance and unconditional love and sacrifice. She taught me that everybody has their own journey through tough decision making in this life. She taught me that although we don't ask for challenges to come in our pathway (in fact, we pray for just the opposite) we do the best we can with what difficulties we face whether self-induced or brought on by the hands of another. My Mom is a rock and in her more mature stature, I enjoy the times we spend these days just talking. Mom, I hope you know how much I've always loved and respected you. Thank you for fulfilling the role God orchestrated for you to be in my life. I would not be who I am today without you!!

By Althea Lanier (ALANI)

~ Mother ~

Lord I thank you this day

For the unique experience of having a mother

Such as ours

That we, her children

Can continue to live our lives

With her example as our guide

She was human, yes, very much so

In her love for others

There was so much to show

No matter how hard

It was never too difficult for others to do

Can we be anything but blessed

To have known this great woman

Our beloved mother

We will feel sad that she has departed
For we can't help but feel the loss
But more importantly, we must feel blessed
For having been nurtured by one of God's children, no
less
One cannot plan life on earth except to do the will of God
And for many who knew her it may seem tragic
That she has departed
But God, He knows that she has played her part

So dears, remember the love and caring
That she shared
And let this be the parting memory of
Our dear mother

~ My Mother, My Heroine, My Inheritance ~

Let us start with a brief disclaimer for the benefit of the skeptic and/or critic in our midst.

My parents were not perfect because those do not exist. If I chose to, and sometimes in my life I have, I could write out a pretty long list of their shortcomings. Thankfully, I have gained some wisdom over the years and realized that in spite of their shortcomings, I had the best parents a girl could ask for. I believe they were divinely chosen just for me.

So this piece is not just to express my thankfulness for my parents, mother particularly, but also to praise my God.

As I grow and mature, hopefully growing in wisdom, I learn to appreciate and give thanks for my parents and the heritage they gave me. As a result I have understood that any material wealth left behind is of little value compared to the memorable, intrinsic care and teaching born of a deep love demonstrated in so many ways. Even though this section is dedicated to my mother, both my parents contributed to the formation and building of my character and get credit for much that I could be complemented for. They are top of the list of my many blessings.

So often we look to the media personalities for symbols of wealth. We spend too much time envying others' material possessions, concluding they are the fortunate ones, the lucky ones. In truth one can have all the trappings of wealth but be very poor in love, the most valuable gift of all.

My parents demonstrated that the truly wealthy are the givers of this world. They gave of their time, talent, skills, emotions, resources etc., they loved without requiring any payment in return. They did it because they serve a loving and powerful God whom they endeavored to obey.

The Random House dictionary of the English language describes wealth as a great quantity of store of money, valuable possessions, property, or other riches. It also defines wealth as an abundance of profusion of anything; plentiful amount. My parents made me feel wealthy by giving me an abundance of love. A richness of sacrificial provision for my welfare; plentiful quality time that made me feel I was not only important to them but special.

I often think of my mother as one of those women who were born to be a mother. Nurturing came naturally to her and she raised her thirteen children and then some (nieces, nephews, cousins), and touched the lives of countless others. I hope everyone have the opportunity to meet and have a relationship with such a woman. She proved that our capacity for loving others is limited only by our willingness to act, to love. Many called her 'Mam' and experienced that nurturing experience not restricted to her biological children. She gave a plentiful supply of love and encouragement coupled with instilling a sense of responsibility. Her capacity for loving others and encouraging them by seeing and expecting the best in them was constantly demonstrated. She applied this to all young people who came into her life. Mam was good at building you up, letting you know in direct and indirect ways that she believed in you.

At my mother's knees I learnt many profound lessons:

- That material goods are transient and fleeting but family and good friends are invaluable and should be nurtured and treated as such. Whenever she was in need she appealed to her God to care for her need. When He answered, she knew of others who were also needy and shared with them. These occasions are etched in my memory; a prayer for a protein source to complete the meal (she was big on balanced meals) – the arrival of a fisherman or butcher at her door – watching her divide into sections the supply she had just received – being sent on an errand to deliver that unsolicited gift – the response of the recipient – thankfulness. To this date, for me the gift that I receive the most satisfaction and blessing from is the one that is unexpected and fills a real need.

- Real wealth increases, it can be invested, and is not affected by the Wall Street market or natural disasters, etc. When I meet people of varying ages who share with me the impact my parents life had on their own, I understand the investment part. I have been able to receive the trust of strangers based on the reputation of my parents – that's an heir receiving return on her parents' investment.

- The wealth to ne valued is not purchasable, it is invaluable. It is not just property; it appreciates undeterred by the circumstances. Is not always comfortable, in fact often difficult, but it is always building, it helps you grow and for me it is a valuable inheritance.

My mother's devotion to us was tangible. She was fully involved and contributed significantly to my life even though my worldly education went beyond her own. This was no easy task, considering she had thirteen of us but for her it was worth it? ** I am often awed and humbled when I reflect on what I inherited of supreme value. I learned to value people over things; that things only mattered if you were able to share them with loved ones. I learned that loving someone often meant exercising 'tough love.' I learned that being unselfish and giving of yourself often had much greater rewards than focusing on self. I learned that the ability to say no or yes honestly without being offensive was one of the most important aspects of personal freedom. Even though we sometimes thought my mother took on more than she should, I have not met someone who could say no more graciously.

I was blessed with a mother who was self-reliant, generous and skillful. She truly believed that learning to take care of oneself (male or female) was paramount to having the ability to provide for self and help another. Caring for yourself meant being able to cook, clean, wash etc. no exceptions for her children whether male or female. She would say that if you were in a bind, working for someone in the capacity of a cook or housekeeper could be an honorable option until you achieved your goal. "There is no shame in work," she often said, "but there is shame in idleness." My parents embodied a wealth of knowledge abilities and skills which they passed on to their kids during their lifetime so that to this day we have an incredible legacy of talents which I pray we can pass on to our children.

My basic needs were always met, often beyond my expectation. Many years ago my older sister was editing an essay I had written for application to a university and noted a statement that I had written to the effect that "even though we could have been considered poor by the world's standard, I never felt poor." She emphatically reminded me that our family **was never poor.** She went on to point out that we never lacked for anything. In fact we always had enough to share with someone less fortunate. I have never forgotten that conversation. It was added to the archive of so many more insightful conversations that I have accumulated during interaction with my family, starting with my wise parents and continuing on with my siblings. The neat discovery along the way has been that many of those wise words and principles are actually found in the Bible.

Self-expression was encouraged with no tolerance of disrespect of the other person. 'Mam' always emphasized that there is room for more than one successful person in a group, family, class, country etc.

Our parents gave us a sense of security that we could rely on them for support and that we were an important part of their life. They provided an environment where learning and growing was encouraged, curiosity understood and enthusiasm applauded. My mother had a special place in her heart for teachers and she did not hesitate to vocalize this. It is a tribute to her influence that ten of her thirteen children were teachers at some point in their working life.

My parents are one my greatest blessings and my mother continues to be top of the list of strong wise women in my life whom I try to emulate. I learned so much from her, that I feel that if I can pass on to my children a few of those lessons I will have done her proud. My mother believed that you should prepare your children for life and they will not only find but be able to make the most of the opportunities. As Mama used to say, "You teach your children to fish and they will never go hungry."

My wealthy inheritance is imbedded in the practical manifestation of a deep belief in God and his promises, trusting God implicitly, using God's material blessings wisely, and generously sharing what you're blessed with both in terms of material gains as well as gifts and abilities freely with others.

My dear mother showed me by example how invaluable moments with loved ones are, how to be thankful. My only regret is that I did not have time to tell her all the things I loved and appreciated about her. For those who still have your mother with you, please don't miss the opportunity to express your love, in words and deeds... forgive, don't sweat the small stuff...it's the love that's most valuable.

~ A Song For Mama ~

Several years ago on Mother's Day, Mama sent me a CD that had been performed by the youth in her church. She didn't know and I still haven't found out who the author is, but I love the words so much and want to share it here. It says so much about parents, especially mothers who wonder daily where the next meal is coming from, living from paycheck to paycheck. This song embodies all mothers everywhere who gives 110% evey day to make sure their children are safe and fed. The sacrifices they make with a smile sometimes and even forgetting to take care of themselves, says a lot about how deep their love flows. I just want to say 'Thanks Ma, for your thoughtfulness" and I want to share this in honor of all mothers everywhere.

Mama Don't Cry No More

1. Mama, hold faith nah man, listen Mama

All things work out for those who love God.

Remember that I love you Mama, and God love you too

Just be strong Mama, tings **MUST** get better. Listen...

CHORUS: (a) O Mama, don' want you to cry no more

Lord Jesus will find another open door

Wipe your tears, don't you ever have no fears,

Father will find a way from out of no where

(b) O Papa don' want you to cry no more

Lord Jesus will find another open door

Wipe your tears, don't you ever have no fears,

Father will find a way from out of no where

2. So, we are children of the light

We walk by faith and we don't walk by sight

We are children of the day, we not children of the night

Our steps are ordered by the Lord Jesus Christ.

Me tell them say, look how many things they have done

to us

They prosecute we daily, but we still don't give up

We are broke, but we love them and we don't get corrupt

Well them is rough and tough

Papa is working, but it's far too much

Sometimes it hurt Mama, hurt, but hush

Don't let the things of the world get to us

Den me tell dem,

3. Mama, on the Word of God, we have to anchor our
faith

Hold on to the promises and hang on to His grace

Speak in tongues, even when we see no food 'pon we
plate

But what is from the Father we most appreciate

We won't suffer, when we trust in the most High

It don' make sense to curl up in a corner and cry

Mama, Mama please wipe the tears from your eyes

Blessed Mama

(Author unknown)

~ Honoring Adwina Barclay ~

Our mother Adwina Barclay is an awesome human being who will do anything in her power to help another person. She is gentle, kind, giving, strong and one of the most caring person you will ever have the pleasure of knowing. Our mom believes God with all of her might and have taught my sister and I to trust and believe God for every and anything our hearts desires. Mom you are a beautiful person inside and out. We cannot thank God enough for putting you into our lives. Your love is irreplaceable.

Sanelle Evans

April 2nd, 2016

~ Our Everything ~

Ma...our everything...TRULY...- our mother, father, sister, friend, lawyer, spiritual mentor. We are eternally grateful to have you in our lives. We may not always express our love in obvious ways, but we need you to know that you are deeply loved.

Thank you Ma for all your love and support; and continuing to stand in the gap for us.

We love you!

Kima Golda Fern Cumberbatch-Chitolie (grand-daughter) & Gibson Chitolie (husband)

Kimson Max Chitolie (great grandson)

~ *What My Mother Has Shown Me* ~

As a mother as far back as I can remember my mother has always shown me unconditional love and what it is to love some else more than yourself.

As a wife she has shown me that a marriage takes God in the midst, love, work, commitment, sacrifice and with the right person it can be one of life's greatest experiences.

As a Christian women she has shown me that God should be my foundation in all things and if I love and put him first I will always be victorious.

Because of all the things my mother has shown and instilled in me I am truly blessed and thankful to God to have given me such a precious jewel as my mother.

Carmetta (Cindy) Williams
April5th, 2016

~ Blessings On Blessings to Mom ~

Love lifted me! It grew and grew in my heart.

Mommy's nurturing spirit filled me from the start

Her endearing love is spread throughout

But the love she gives me makes me shout

Although she didn't have it easy and things were not

perfect

Standing, standing she's strong and sweet

Continuing on without a feat!

It's with God's grace Mommy's a rock star,

Shining and shining through it all.

With a bright light, a divine wonderful woman

Blooming and growing more and more with fullness

For this is where her five daughters get it from

Kind, nurturing spirits shared upon all.

With all my love, Tine.

Christine Perkins and family

April 10th, 2016

~*Mom* ~

(Roberta Lucenius)

You passed from this earth too early, leaving heartbreak
in your wake.

Every day, I see your delicate facial features in many
faces I pass.

Your expressive eyes screamed kindness and depth.

Depth you couldn't show living the generation you did.

You were a quiet, gentle woman, an observer, with a
selfless soul.

Truly, the wind beneath so many wings.

You were our rock, believer in all things good, our
cheerleader in life.

Your death changed life for many, your endless well of
support and love faded.

I wish I knew then how one way your world was. It was
all about us.

Did anyone ever ask you how you were doing…were you
having a good day?

As our true north, we tapped into you for our every need.

Why didn't I know more about you…as a woman?

You pointed me in the direction of success with your belief in my potential.

I followed your script…I wanted to make you proud.

I needed to find my own script. Your death gave me no choice.

As a pleaser - with no one now to please, I blazed my own trail.

With many years gone by, I feel your gentle wind still guiding me, especially as a Mom.

Your words are my words to my child. I wish she felt the warmth of your loving eyes.

Life lessons you left are many. The gift of non-judgement and fairness first.

But most importantly, you taught me the need to be taken seriously as a woman, because you weren't.

Cynthia (Cindy) Lucenius-Schick
April 5, 2016

~ Tribute To Our Mother ~

Janet Magdaline Eugene

(Janzo)

What a perfect opportunity to share our thoughts of you on Mother's Day. Our wellbeing always came first. There are simply no words to express how much we miss you. It would be so easy to use a few beautiful words like classy, loving, determined, strong, compassionate, and stylish to describe your personality. However, your actions day after day were what really conveyed the true essence of you.

We remember all so well….and still laugh about it…

- Your undying love for music. In true Janzo style, your whistling and singing at the top of your lungs, (anything to wake us up) really early in the morning, the songs from choir rehearsal from the night before

- Dancing in the living room on a Sunday afternoon, listening to the old greats like Ella Fitzgerald, Sara Vaughn, Frank Sinatra, Dean Martin, Tony Bennett, Eartha Kitt, Miriam Makeba (Pata Pata), and big band music like Glen Miller and others

- Making sure our family was fed three meals each day with snacks in between

- Your love for driving at top speed

- Your creativity in the kitchen: who would think; one egg with scallions, milk, and can of corned beef for a delicious omelet to feed eight.

- Tirelessly working to have our school uniforms washed and ironed and ready for school

- Your bright ideas: Your resilience in planning and eventually opening your own preschool (St Michael's Preschool) that was well recognized and made such an impact on preschoolers in Dominica for over 20 years
- Sketching your clothing designs and having best friend Mrs. Guye make them on a budget
- Your love for the arts: performing in local musical productions like Porgy and Bess and others
- Your deep relationship with God our Creator, and love for family

We appreciate all your efforts over the years and cannot thank you and daddy enough for being such wonderful parents and role models to us.

#prayingwoman   #bestmotherever   #incrediblerolemodel
#onehellofawoman   #alwaysinourhearts
Ann Denton
April 5th, 2016

~ *Ephesians 4:32* ~

Ephesians 4:32 (KJV) *"And be ye kind one to another, tenderhearted, forgiving one another, even as God for Christ's sake hath forgiven you."*

That is the first Bible verse I remember Mama teaching us. With six children – 4 headstrong girls and 2 younger boys trying to be in charge, you can imaging the chaos and wrestling matches going on regularly. Mama made sure we knew that even when we fought and argued – at the end of the day we were 'blood' and needed to be forgiving and be there for each other.

You would think that once we were all grown up, we would be the best....well, not so much. One always does or says something to 'annoy' another or tries to give advice or just want to prove they're better than the other. But, thankfully because Mama instilled that verse in us and it's etched on our brain, we try to endeavor to do just that – forgive one another – not perfect but we keep working on it.

As of this writing, Mama has twelve

grandchildren, and eleven great grandchildren; it amazes me that she remembers everyone's birthday. The first call they will get on the morning of their birthday is Mama calling to say or sing "Happy Birthday." I know they will remember that for years every time her name comes up.

We quickly learned over the years that if you want to call Mama to say "hello" make sure you have at least forty-five minutes to one hour to spare. Don't for one minute think you will call and get away with "Hi Ma, just a quick call..." Mama, always so eager to catch up on what's new or going on in her children lives – and that includes grandchildren and great grandchildren as well, wants an almost minute by minute detail of each life. Then she takes everything back to scripture to remind them to obey their parents, to remind us to "train up a child in the way that he should go." Many times that would include a mini prayer service while you're thinking "O boy, maybe I should have called her when I had more time."

At times we try to very gently remind Mama that her children and even her grandchildren are all grown up. Mama in turn reminds us firmly that we are still her children and grown up or not, we still need to be reminded of God's Word. Now, who can argue with that??

Mama, her name is Mary – named after the mother of Jesus.

M - ama, it's been a long, hard but blessed journey

A - gain and again you overcame by God's grace

R - esilient, you've been holding on to your faith

Y - ou've made it to your 80's and counting...

Candia Cumberbatch-Lucenius
April 13th, 2016

Mama's children and grandchildren are giving her 'flowers' to enjoy while she can. Trying to put it all into words is challenging and overwhelming. Some seem to be at a loss for words, but each had something to say.

~*Mama's Travels*~

Mama thankfully has had the privilege to travel a few times and one of her granddaughters Tamilia Maria (named for Mama) Dolor, put together a presentation of Mama's travels. I pray it blesses her and others as we take a walk, or plane ride down and around memory lane.

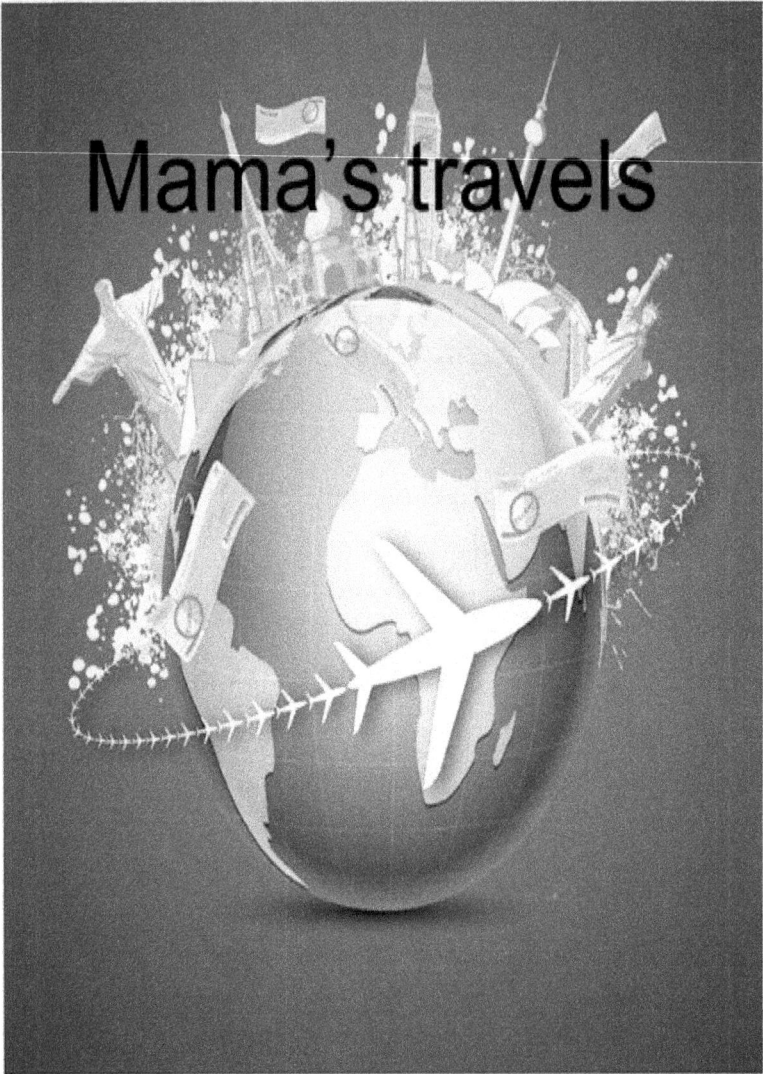

Mama's travels

United Kingdom

City and County of the City of London
South East, England, United Kingdom

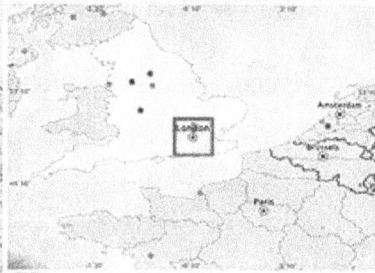

maphill

© 2011 Maphill

London museum

Canterbury

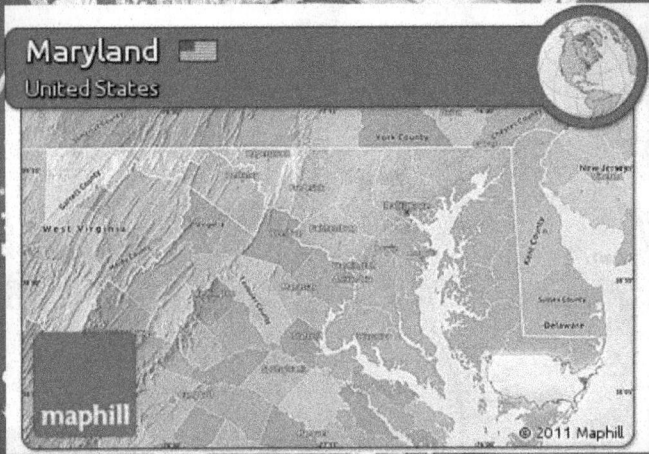

The US of A

Maryland
United States

maphill

© 2011 Maphill

The US of A

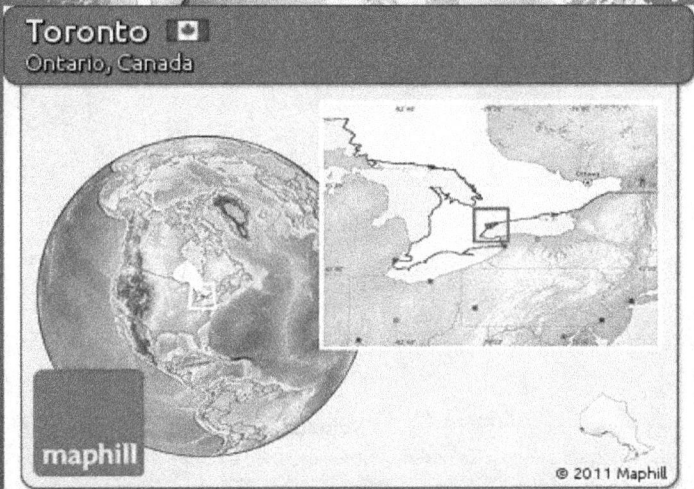

Canada - Mama has been to Toronto

Toronto 🇨🇦
Ontario, Canada

maphill

© 2011 Maphill

Put together by your grand-daughter -
Tamilia ^_^

~ Mama Cumberbatch ~

I will refer to the lady being spoken about in this passage as Mama Cumberbatch. Her actual name is Mary Maximilia Cumberbatch. Funny - when we were children, I knew her as Marie Cumberbatch- but we grew up in St Lucia and all kinds of versions of your name turn up as you grow up. For example, I knew myself as Karen - I grew up, required a passport and discovered I was not Karen after all but Karan- but that's St Lucia.

But this is about Mama Cumberbatch who is my mother - still alive and literally 'kickin'. I want to thank God for her legacy especially because I consider her example extremely significant in our family. You see

Mama grew up at one end of our lovely island home and began a nursing career after high school. She then married a policeman - my father - (gave up her nursing career) and had 2 children - myself and my older sister - all at that end of the island where all her family had been for whatever generations.

When we were still toddlers, she followed her policeman husband to the other end of the island where she settled and had 4 more children. As we grew up, we discovered the end of the island where she had grown up, discovered our roots, loved it and moved back there - one after the other. I know as I kept going to 'our' end of the island, I resented that other end of the island - but it was 'home.'

But it had been a significant, life-changing move that I can only now fully appreciate- as I grow old. For in that end of the island, a Mama was introduced to Jesus, accepted Him as her personal Saviour - decided to follow Him and never turned back.

And she introduced her children to that wonderful Saviour. I have never been the same.

Mama and Daddy's relationship was on and off since I was young and the Evangelical church that Mama had become a member of, was very supportive as she practically became a single Mum of 6 children with sporadic visits from Daddy and very little financial assistance.

She changed careers and became a teacher (quite successfully). She qualified as a teacher but the family demands hindered any further progress she might have made. Years later, I also became a teacher.

We grew up with morning devotions. Sunday school and church and were taught the ways of the one and only true God. We attended Sunday school, all church services and as we grew older became members of the church youth group; with church camp during the long holidays.

I followed the Lord in baptism and began to teach Sunday School when I was 12 years old. On finishing secondary school, I attended Bible College for two years before embarking on my teaching career. I consider these events life changing and important to shaping me into the individual I've become. I consider my childhood a very happy time and I believe it was all due to the love that I found in Jesus as a child. Thank you Mama for the Jesus legacy – it is the most important above all.

Karan Lillian Mary Cumberbatch-Casabianca

April 11th, 2016

~Mothers Feel The Pain ~

I think it is fitting to include here a song by one of our local calypsonians from St. Lucia – Jaunty Regis; another of my favorites. Jaunty's inspiration for writing this song is that he basically raised his first two daughters by himself. This brought the realization of how hard a mother's job really is. Not that their mother was absent, but she was young and learning.

Mothers Feel The Pain

Anytime a woman attracts a man

To get her he will try everything he can.

O yes, he will spend for she

Give she plenty money

And play the sleekest games

Anytime he hear the word pregnancy

Right away he pretend that he don't know she

All on she own she left to decide

Cause she know this big belly she can't hide.

Say when a father neglect his kid

And this kid is in the need

There is hungry belly to feed

Mother's feel the pain, the pain

So many fathers are having fun

While their children are on the run

No one gives them a helping hand

Mothers feel the pain, the pain

Now hear this, mothers raising a family

Without the help of a father

Keep up the good works

Take heed little ones

Mothers are working from nine to five

Trying their best to stay alive

Plenty of mouths to feed, Lord what a dread to heed

No one to help them out, with all them plenty mouth

Never judge a woman by what she does

Find out the reason for her demise

Sometimes this thing does send them insane

Only the mothers feel the pain, the pain

Take example little ones, and always love your mother

Remember the hard times; just she and she alone

Never judge a woman by what she does

Find out the reason for her demise

Time after time, she's burdened with shame

Only the mothers feel the pain

Remember the nice things Mommy used to buy you

Always remember the hardship

Calypsonian Jaunty Regis

~ Deep Love ~

In my research for contributions to this book of tributes to mothers, including my own mother Mama, I found that so many of us have a complex relationship with our mothers. Almost everyone was at a loss for words, even the most eloquent speakers had difficulty putting words to what they wanted to say to or about their mothers. The one constant was that everyone spoke of love – that deep love that only a connection between a mother and child can make possible.

So, what caused us all to stall when searching for the right words? Not sure about anyone else, but for me it was a little overwhelming. How do you put into words over 59 years of such complex feelings of love, anger, curiosity, sadness, respect, and trying to understand what made Mama tick?

My conclusion – I just love her – she's the only mother I have and will ever have. It's so easy to think, why did Mama do or say certain things? Mama was not perfect, but she tried her best with what she had, keeping

God and His Word as her standard. Some of her decisions regarding her family and six children was made after misguided, maybe well-meaning advice from some friends and others. Over the years I've learned to forgive these "miserable comforters," in part because I needed to release any hurt and some anger I felt regarding some of the decisions Mama made based on their advice. But mainly because I look back on some of my decisions and realize that I wasn't perfect, made some mistakes as well – in raising my children and in the decisions I made for their lives. And if God can forgive me, who am I not to be forgiving as well. Again, remember Mama's favorite verse to teach her children?

Ephesians 4:32 And be ye kind one to another, tender hearted, forgiving one another, even as God for Christ sake hath forgiven you.

~ A Day in the Life of Mama ~

Hardworking, tireless, sleepless at times
She's up and working without waking us up
"Come on. It's time to go" we hear Mama call
Jumping out of bed and racing for the shower.

One shower, six children how did we do it?
Mama has breakfast ready so one less thing to do
Our uniforms pressed, and hanging up neatly
The school books stacked so we can't miss them.

At last we're out the door, and off to school we go
We start the mile walk across the field
Laughing and playing with others we meet on the way
Determined to make our day the best one ever.

At the end of the day, as we make the walk back home
As the questions of "wonder what's for dinner?"
Played over and over in our heads
The hunger grew harder to ignore the closer we got.

Surprise!! As we got to the house, the smell of dinner

Yeah11I guess we won't be starving we think

God has provided again, not sure how He did it

But Mama was thankful we won't go to bed hungry

Many times over the years, we remind ourselves that God has always provided. I cannot remember ever going to bed with nothing to eat – some days the meal was smaller than others, but the need was always met. **Psalm 37:25** *I have been young, and now am old; yet have I not seen the righteous forsaken, nor his seed begging bread.*

~Mothers Are a Gift from God~

M = is for Mom…Every mother is not a Mom. A mom is someone who God has given to her children like a gift; a mom is Magnificent, Marvelous, and Magical…My mom was my BEST FRIEND!

O **= is for Outstanding**…My mom was an OUTSTANDING woman who feared God. She was one of the most Influential and Smartest ladies I have ever known. She was extremely wise and full of life and loved her children endlessly. My mom was a very unselfish woman who always put her family (children) in front of her.

T **= is for Tough**…Although being a Mom is tough, my Mom was a gentle soul with a soft heart and a tough mind. My mom was "Strong" and "Tough" when she needed to be especially when protecting her children.

H **= is for Healing**…Every time I hurt myself, fell, or

even got my feelings hurt; my Mom knew exactly what to do and say to make me feel better. She had a "healing" touch and a smile that was infectious. She always made me feel better even when I was wrong. Everything she did and said was always with Love and she never made me feel bad and showed me Love even when I made mistakes.

E = **is for Encouraging**…My mom always had encouraging words for me especially when I was feeling sad or depressed. She knew how to lift my spirits when no one else could. She was always positive and had many words of wisdom and encouragement.

R = **is for Righteous**. My mom was a woman of God who was righteous in her walk with Jesus Christ. She wasn't perfect and she would say that often and she also said "But I serve a perfect God." (Matthew 6.33)

My Mother or Mom left her children too soon, but God wanted her more. I know she is in Heaven and smiling down on me. I can feel her presence every day; she lives in my heart. I miss her smile, her laughter, her touch, and most of all her Love and Friendship. She is now free and has followed the path God made for her.

This is my love letter to my mother who was a God-fearing woman and sacrificed for her children everyday of her life. She left us too soon, but she is now free…free of pain, grief, and free to be in Heaven with God and she has found peace at the end of the road….

I dedicate this tribute for Mother's Day to my Mother, Doris Elizabeth Britton who was my "Hero" and my "Best Friend" and truly an angel who is now resting in Heaven. I love you Mommie…..One day we will meet again in heaven……God Bless….

Your Daughter, Dawn Elizabeth Britton

April 12th, 2016

~ Tribute to Carol Cuthbert Charles ~

My mother, Carol Cuthbert Charles (Frazer) was born in Saint Lucia- she is going to be 82 years old in April 2016. She did what is unheard of today birthed 9 girls and 4 boys without epidural --over half of them are now in their 50's.....I understand most were home birthed. My mother career was mothering/ parenting all her life. Today she is also a grandmother to over 23 and great grandmother to 7.

We were raised with strong Christian values and beliefs...dedicating your children to God was a must in her faith. When you look for a mother with core values such as being your brother's keeper, feeding the hungry, caring for the sick, praying without ceasing, giving you her all at all times, believing that humans will stumble, but please give a helping hand up. .....my mother is that Christian mother, soldier. We have in her as children- a nurse, teacher, chef, house administrator, wardrobe designer, interior decorator, gardener, produce expert, old traditional medicinal specialist, ...a list that can go on and on...as you can tell a complete multi-talented mother.

What we as children have come to realize as we have children and grandchildren of our own- this role of mother is not for the weak...you can only read some of the headlines in the news and realize giving birth does not give you the blue print for mothering. I believe she did it with God by her side- that is the only way you raise 13 children, grandchildren, great grandchildren, nieces, nephews, God-children- take care of her own siblings who say thank you forever-Over and over again.

Today in the words of Maya Angelo- we salute the "phenomenal woman" that Carol Charles is. She accepted the mother role and did as if she had a doctorate in that field- I would say life experience has given her all the great titles....She was schooled by praying for guidance by putting all her needs before God.

We give thanks Mamie Carol Charles. We all give thanks- the day God chose you for us!

Noella Charles

April 12th, 2016

~ A Son's Tribute ~

The following poem is submitted by my son Swanson in honor of Mama and his mother.

Seems like it says what so many of us would like to say to our mothers.

Dear Mother

I'm writing you to tell you that I love you

Something I hardly ever do.

I never tell you enough how much I love you

and it's something I must do.

I need to let you know mother how much

You really mean to me so I'm telling you now

you mean the world to me.

I need to thank you for all you do for me.

Your unconditional love toward me means a lot to me.

You've never turned your back

on me and I know it's something you'll never do.

Anytime I need someone to talk to

You're always there to help me through

And anytime I need a favor you always seem

To be there, too. There's nothing in this

world that I could do to pay you back for all you do.

When God gave me to you,

That's the best thing he could ever do,

So this poem is dedicated to you

Because I don't know how else to say Thank You.

© *2009 Herman Vymislicky*

Published on April 2009

~ A Mother's Work ~

A mother's work is never done; no matter what they say

She carries her child for nine months inside

Then another year at least on the outside.

The years go by, and they grow up

Who do they turn to when they have their own?

A mother's work is never done; she helps raise

grandchildren too

Just when she thinks she can take a break, here come the

great grandchildren.

Candia Cumberbatch-Lucenius

April 12th, 2016

~ Tribute to Roberta Ann Lucenius ~

My Mom, Roberta Ann Lucenius, was born Roberta Ann Matson. Every childhood memory I have of her includes either a smile, laughter, or some moment of wisdom where she helped me out somehow, usually from being in trouble with my Dad. One thing was always certain, that she gave me her loving support in whatever I did. This included packing a small bag when I wanted to run away from home (at age 6), sending me off with a smile, knowing I would be back in a short while, which I was of course.

Much of my adult life, with the confidence in God that I have, I can attribute to my Mom. She was sure to take us to church each Sunday, whether or not we wanted to go, and made sure we knew, to her best, who God was and that we were loved. Her love and her heart for God has stuck with me, and for that I am very, very thankful. She was our spiritual backbone growing up, and it has impacted all of us kids in meaningful ways.

Looking back on it now, she did a lot more than just smile and take us to church. She cooked meals for years, did the grocery shopping, cleaned the house, was a great wife to our Dad, and still managed to get to all of our practices, games, track meets, and whatever event was important at the time. At the time I know we said "thanks Mom", but it is only years later that I can appreciate all that she did for us on a daily basis.

The amazing thing is that she did things outside of the home as well. In addition to holding down a job at times while we were growing up, she, along with my Dad, ran the Miss Burlington County Scholarship Pageant for many years. In addition to the County pageant, she also was a part of the Miss New Jersey Pageant, and chaperoned several of the winning girls to the Miss America Pageant. Even today, I enjoy watching the Miss America Pageant, and the wonderful memories of my Mom it brings.

Sadly, my Mom died in 1990, but not without a final, wonderful, only what Mom can do moment. I was in the Navy, away in Operation Desert Storm, and not able to come home, or so it was thought. She was in the final stages of ovarian cancer, and everyone in the family told her that I would not be able to make it home to see her one last time. Against all odds, I got the permission, flew home from the mid-east, and made it home. At the time she had not sat up for weeks, and was very very weak, still insisting that I'll be there. When I walked in the room, to everyone's amazement, she sat up, her eyes cleared a bit, and we had a nice, long, and quiet talk just the two of us. I let her know how much I appreciated everything she did, and how much I loved her and always would. We prayed together, laughed together, cried together, and affirmed with confidence that we would see each other again at the return of Christ.

I am thankful to our God for the life of my Mom, her heart for all of us kids, the wife and mother she was, and for each and every moment she made us happy, try harder, of just feel better about being a person in this world.

Jon Scott Lucenius
April 12th, 2016

~ Mama's Legacy ~

Mama turns 82 on April 25th 2016, and as I look back on her life and remember the legacy she has built, it blesses me and I'm proud to call her my mother. I recently reminded her of that in one of our recent conversations. Her children and grandchildren are teachers, nurses, very impressive knack for cooking (even though not professional), a bursa, sales, phlebotomist, some bachelor, masters and one PhD qualified. Her first great grand-child is already a high school graduate and enrolled in college. Another great grandchild receives awards and recognitions too numerous to mention in music – Kimson plays the piano, guitar and violin and has a beautiful amazing voice as well. He excels academically as well. Jemini has consistently stayed on the honor roll throughout elementary, middle and now high school. She was even awarded the Presidential Honor for Academic Excellence one year.

As Mama looks around at all the accomplishments of her family, I pray she sees her life as a success and embraces the legacy her life has been. These are all many bunches of the flowers Mama so wants to enjoy while she still can. I'm not sure exactly, but I think I can trace Mama's love for flowers to when her father (her best friend and love of her life) died. Mama speaks of being so over-whelmed at the funeral that she fainted. She dreamt she was running in a field of the most beautiful flowers, and her father was in a boat beckoning her to him.

~ Winifred Thecla McMillan ~

September 23, 1921- August 2011

Mummy knew how to suffer and to endure

Not only physical pain but emotional and mental to the

end

She was never one to complain or to mourn

Her faith and trust in God brought her great consolation

She prayed many, many prayers; she hummed many

tunes of griefs and burden

She took all to the Lord in prayer with sighs and cries

and silent prayers

Mummy was very wise, for she pondered many things in

her heart.

God was her confident, her advocate and her judge

This she knew without a doubt

Well done Mummy, God is pleased with you.

Mummy was never a scholar; never went to a university

But was the most dedicated and thorough teacher

She taught with her voice, her hands and her eyes

By her gestures, her tears, her love and her endurance

Mummy was a strong woman, persevering and kind

She battled through life's challenges and endured to the

end.

Mummy performed many duties, of which she never

grew weary or abandoned her role

As chief cook and bottle washer, home keeper, caregiver

and nurturer

Mother, wife, sister, friend and neighbor - Her doors

were constantly opened to everyone

And although her house was full; she always had room

for another one

She gave from her heart of the little she had; no one went

hungry as they passed by

She was a gift from God and humanity

Who gave birth to one dozen siblings, of whom eight are

among us

Mummy has touched thousands of lives directly and

indirectly

She gave us love, she gave us strength, and she gave us
courage to persevere

You are gone but will never be forgotten

We know we will meet again in your Heavenly domain

To share laughter and joy and to praise God together

Life has never been the same without you

Rest in the arms of Jesus, since you had a long and
tiresome journey

Happy Mothers' day mummy. Memories of you will
never be forgotten

Rest in peace

You're loving Daughter

Lucian McMillan- Cardona
April 12th, 2016

~ Tribute to Janie Louise Miles ~

Born 06/03/1951

From Easton, PA

She was a very kindhearted person and very giving to her family and friends. She loved to study God's Word and share her testimony with everyone around her. She was also a very loving wife and mother.

Ladina Miles-Stewart

April 13th, 2016

~ *Wayne's Tribute* ~

"But there's a story behind everything. How a picture got on a wall. How a scar got on your face. Sometimes the stories are simple, and sometimes they are hard and heartbreaking. But behind all your stories is always your mother's story, because hers is where yours begin." — Mitch Albom, For One More Day

I came across this quote and felt it was a fitting way to begin this tribute. The story of this Cumberbatch

Family begins with Mary, Marie (who we always thought she was), Hellis (her childhood house name), Ma Combie (how she is known to her closest friends), Mrs. Cumberbatch (how everybody else knows her) and Mama to us. Her story as it relates to us is one of much sacrifice but also one of extreme faith and Godliness. I have always described Mama as the Godliest person I have ever met. Hers is a life of complete commitment to her God. All aspects of her life relates to her faith in God and that has been the driving force in her life from as long as I know. So for Mama no matter, the adversity, no matter the disappointment, in times of joy and victory in times of plenty (of which we hardly experienced) and in times of little or none (often times we had to endure) we were always taught to give God the glory and praise.

Mama was a wonderful teacher and we know as she taught all of us and the stories of her teaching we get to hear from the many people who recall their days at the Plain View School. The people she taught with, the many students she helped learn to read and write all give that story of her extraordinary work as a teacher. It makes us all proud to have had a mother like that. As in all things hers was also a life sacrifice – sacrifice for us her six children. Having to raise us virtually on her own, caring nurturing and mentoring us to become well rounded citizens. We probably didn't all live up to her expectations but as a good mother she has continued to show love to all of us. The story of the Cumberbatch family is long, interesting, sad, and joyful, has moments of surprise, has moments of disappointment, has moments of celebration, has moments of pain and has moments of happiness. Despite it all it, is our story and behind it all, is a wonderful mother who loved us all. Mary Cumberbatch, Marie, Hellis, Ma Combie, Mrs.Cumberbatch, Mama - WE LOVE YOU.

Mama I love you. Wayne

~ My Remarkable Mother ~

Mother is a remarkable woman. She was as only child born to parents who came from large families. Many of her summers were spent with her cousins in the country. She had three girlfriends, all the way through high school to this very day. When it came to dating, most of the time they came as a "package deal"—if you dated one, often it was with the understanding that the others came along. A different day and time! The declaration of war in December 1940 took a heavy toll: many boys in her senior çlass graduated early and enrolled in the armed services. Girls married and/or worked at a young age in those Depression, war-time years.

My parents met in the summer of 1942. While hanging out at the Pier, the local amusement park, with one of her friends, they were approached by two sailors. As the story goes, one told the other that he had dibs on the blonde...yep, my mother! To make it even funnier, my future-father worked on a merchant ship with her uncle, who had been trying, without success, to get him to meet his pretty niece…this uncle had also been trying to get her to meet a nice young sailor in his ship!

"They married four years later. Their "dating" consisted of being together seven times, plus many, many letters. And thus began their 35 years of marriage and her 31+ years as a Navy wife.

And therein lies my reason for calling her "remarkable". During all those years, she exhibited resilience, endurance, perseverance, lack of complaining, resourcefulness … as she does to this day. Why do I say this?

Well, as a Navy wife, every two years she became head of household, mother *and* father. In the Navy one had sea-duty every two years. During that time, Daddy might be gone 6-9 months of *each* of those two years. Oh, sure, there were letters, but they were weeks in coming. No cell phones in those days, so you *might* get a call once or twice while he was at sea or in a faraway port.

Eventually three children were added to the mix: me in 1946, Bill in 1948, and John in 1955. As I said, she took on all the functions of both parents. Of all my memories of those years, none were of her complaining, no tears, no bemoaning her fate. If those things occurred, she never showed it. She carried on, did what needed to be done.

In 1950 we were assigned duty in California. They drove across the country from Texas, in a convertible, no A/C, 2 kids in underwear! Two months later I came down with polio. After two days of fever Mother got a neighbor to watch Bill, got on a bus, with me in her arms, for the ride to the hospital. Daddy was overseas and couldn't come home for a week. For that week *she* was the one making all the decisions pertaining to my care. I was in the hospital for a little over a year, but look in our family photo albums, and you'll always find her smiling with me. Amazing!

Don't get me wrong ... Daddy was an integral part of our family life and upbringing. There was no question who ruled our family, present or not. But Mother held it all together. She raised three children, a lot of it while on her own. She took me to the day-long clinics, waiting for consultations. She managed the finances. She took care of the details of everyday life. Some of this changed

94

when Daddy didn't have sea-duty, but she still kept us all on point! And it continues to this very day.

Even though Mother is now 91, I still find her remarkable! She still is resilient, enduring, persevering, resourceful, and complains little. I draw on her insight and strength quite often. As far as I am concerned, modern women could learn a lot from *her*"

by Sydna Elrod

April 18, 2016

~ *Mama Dearest* ~

He called you Mother Dearest or Mama Dearest and you knew he meant it – not a day went by if he didn't call to check on you. Even after he moved to Barbados to live and get to know Daddy's side of the family better, he still called every day. Sometimes it was because he needed something (smile), but mostly just to say hi.

He was so proud to be seen with you and always relished the times you got to go church together, or just for a walk or just hang out at the beach. He took pride in dressing you up or just critiquing what you wore. Many times he had us screaming out in loud laughter when he exclaimed, "You not going out with me in THAT!!" He then went through your closet and found what he thought was a more appropriate or better matched outfit. He even went shopping on several occasions and bought you something he saw in a store that he thought you would look great it.

I know how much it broke your heart when he left us; it did that to all of us; but you were his Mama Dearest. I remember what you said to me when I told you, "If it hurts me so much, I can't even imagine what you're going through; he was your son – your first boy; no mother should have to bury her child." You replied that after you had four girls, you prayed for a son and God gave you Ralph; after which you then asked God for a brother for him and God gave you Wayne. And as much as it hurt and as much as it broke your heart to lose him, you knew and believed with all your heart that you would see him again when Christ returned. You were confident in that because you knew he had given his life to God, had turned his life around from some of the mistakes and lifestyle he had chosen. You also thanked God for lending Ralph to us. That's the kind of woman you are – giving God thanks and praise was your priority. **I Thessalonians 5:18** "In every thing give thanks: for this is the will of God in Christ Jesus concerning you."

~ What are You Thankful For? ~

What are you thankful for we ask year after year.
What are you thankful for – be honest if you dare.
What are you thankful for – do you struggle to think
What are you thankful for – let's see – as you blink.

I'm thankful for parents and grandparents who tried their best.
I'm thankful for siblings, even the fights and the tests.
I'm thankful for children – and grandchildren who melt our hearts.
I'm thankful for nieces, nephews, cousins, uncles and aunts.

I'm thankful for the laughter, the tears and the sighs.
I'm thankful for the bumps in the road even through the cries.
I'm thankful because they just made me appreciate life's hue.
I'm thankful for friendships – the old and the new.

I'm thankful for family – fun times and all.
I'm thankful for blessings – the big and the small.

I'm thankful for good health, and healing when needed.
I'm thankful for my life and the journey I've weathered.

But most of all, I'm thankful for God's love and His Son
Jesus Christ.
And although I'm not always thankful for everything,
I'm blessed that I can be thankful in everything.

Candia Cumberbatch-Lucenius (An original)
November 26th, 2015

~*Mama*~

Look at you - beautiful at any age

So much love so many memories

Look at you - gorgeous at any age

So much joy and happiness you shared through the years

Look at you - we're so blessed to share this life with you

Don't you ever feel that we don't love you

Don't you ever feel that we don't care

If you only knew how much you mean to us

Look at you - look at you

Everytime I think of you brings a smile to my face

Everytime I see you it brings a smile to my heart

Look at you look at you happy birthday we love you

Makeeva Andrewna Candacey (granddaughter)

April14th, 2016

~ A Dim Reflection on Ten Thousand Kisses ~
Roberta Lucenius

Losing your mother in the teen years is an interesting thing. As an adult, I know that her influence on me is incalculable, but not knowing her as an adult leaves a gap of understanding and the inability to retro-imagine her presence in my life when I was younger. There aren't shared conversations that we were able to have that recapture and perpetuate memories. As the youngest and somewhat of an only child, many days, she was the only person I related to in the home, but there isn't a third party to refer to draw up other memories that lay dormant.

I have always said that my mother's real and tangible love for me made God's love believable to me.

That is a true statement that cannot be watered down. However, I have struggled to add to it as far as her influence over me. Yet, recently, I read a longer biographical interview with Bono and learned about his life with his father after his mother died at a young age during his teens. He reflected on his relationship with his mother in a song called "Iris" from U2's recent album. He associates his mother, "Iris" with what we know of stars.

It has been said that when we see a star go out, it is likely that the effective death of the star was years before. Though the star died, the light that it produced continued to travel through space and time until it reaches us. The absence of that light isn't realized until the last light particle travels the long journey from source to destination.

Bono likens his experience of his mother to a star that is a million miles away. The light is inescapable, but it takes a thousand years to get here. We live in a universe that is beautiful but dark and cold. Before we even realize their effect, mothers are the light and warmth in our lives in a dark and cold world. I think dudes like me enjoy the warmth and the light of their mothers, before we even know that we need warmth and light. Yet when the star goes out, it takes years for the effect of the warmth and the light to go out, even years for us to feel and realize the gap that their presence left. I enjoy the warmth that my mother gave me that lasted beyond her. And in some ways, since this reality is "a thousand years away" though she is gone, I still have not yet experienced the full loss of that warmth.

The other theme that is addressed in the song is that a star brings light into our life. For Bono knowing his mother and feeling her hold him in the darkness somehow reveals to Bono something of who he is. Knowing (or at least remembering) her in the darkness of life somehow helps him know himself. That to me is the catch and the difficulty that I feel I share with Bono. There is something about myself hidden with my mother that I can no longer access, at least on this side of eternity. There is a sadness in this to me that is subtle, but precious because it doesn't stand alone.

What I do know about my mother is what she wanted for all of her kids. She loved to see her loved ones thrive. She lived so to see us live. She did this in such a way that we should live our lives forward, not in reverse. In some ways, as I live my life moving forward, I come to understand her influence on me in retrospect. She loved to mentor younger women. I do too. She loved to coach them to live and to perform (in pageants). I love that too. She would get lost in conversations with others, listening to them share their lives with her. As a pastor, that is sort of my deal, part of the things I do.

Bono reflects on a few of the particular memories and the influence of his mother:

You took me by the hand

I thought that I was leading you

But it was you made me your man

I dream where you are

Iris standing in the hall

She tells me I can do it all

Iris wakes to my nightmares

Don't fear the world it isn't there

Iris playing on the strand

She buries the boy beneath the sand

Iris says that I will be the death of her

It was not me

Iris… Iris…

Free yourself, to be yourself if only you could see

yourself

Free yourself, to be yourself if only you could see…

Bono speaks of the tiny memories, the snapshots in our minds of our mothers and their tiny bits of care and even their complaints of their care (the death of me). These things, in many ways, are the forgettable ways mothers care for us. They are part of the canon of ten thousand kisses that are forgotten but that can never be taken away from us. Their love and their light, though not particularly remembered in detail, give us the ability to free ourselves that we might be ourselves. These tiny acts of care and love are the ways that mothers, at their best, show us how they see us. If we can only see ourselves with the clarity that our mothers once saw us, that love would free us. That is the kind of truth and love that sets us free. Free to be ourselves and free to see ourselves.

Marc Lucenius April 13th, 2016

~ Mama's Prayers ~

Another huge part of Mama's life that I am eternally grateful and thankful for is prayer. Mama often talked about staying on her knees for her children, great and grandchildren. Previously, I mentioned my earliest recollection of Mama calling on the church to help prayer for our sister Karan who had been diagnosed with epilepsy, and I witnessed firsthand how God worked to take care of Karan. Although she never completely stopped having seizures, they were managed with treatment and Karan (thank God) went on to live a very normal live. I have been blessed to share this testimony many times over the years.

Prayer has been a focal point for me and a standard I live my life by. Many years later I had the opportunity to bring to memory Mama's prayer and believing, when our sister Kathleen (Kathee) was told she had a fast growing tumor on her brain, and would need surgery to get it out. She had been complaining of headaches for about 2 years - which nothing seemed to help.

I remember sitting at Kathee's home one night,

watching TV when she suddenly starting crying that she couldn't see – everything was black for about 5 minutes. As expected she was terrified that she was going blind. After some research, my husband and I came across the Hallelujah Acres (a Christian based company in North Carolina), who stressed believing prayer, and daily devotionals to start every day. With help from a few friends and sister Karan we got the funds together and went there for two weeks. By the end of the first week, Kathee woke up on Saturday morning and noticed no headaches for the first time in two years.

After returning home both a CTScan and MRI showed no trace of that tumor. The neurologist couldn't believe it, and wanted to run more test and get second and third opinions. But praise God! He is the same yesterday, today and forever. He still hears us and answers prayer as we go to Him believing – as I learned at Mama's knees.

Another example Mama continues to exhibit is to trust that God is closer than a brother. She lives with the belief that God will protect her and provide for her better than anyone else can; and He has. We have seen it over and over again throughout the years.

So Mama, enjoy your flowers, confident in the knowledge that you are loved and appreciated for all you've done and continue to do. You truly are a strong Godly woman and I am indeed grateful for the foundation of God's Word you gave all your children, grandchildren and great grandchildren. We will continue to endeavor to carry this on with our own children, grandchildren and great grandchildren. May God continue to bless you richly.

For everyone who contributed, let us honor our mothers whether they are still here or not as the Virtuous Woman of Proverbs 31 – as they are – in whole or in part. Remember, our mothers are/were not perfect (neither are we) but they gave their all with what they had or knew and we love them as we know they love(d) us.

Proverbs 31:10-31

10 Who can find a virtuous woman? for her price is far above rubies.

11 The heart of her husband doth safely trust in her, so that he shall have no need of spoil.

12 She will do him good and not evil all the days of her life.

13 She seeketh wool, and flax, and worketh willingly with her hands.

14 She is like the merchants' ships; she bringeth her food from afar.

15 She riseth also while it is yet night, and giveth meat to her household, and a portion to her maidens.

16 She considereth a field, and buyeth it: with the fruit of her hands she planteth a vineyard.

17 She girdeth her loins with strength, and strengtheneth her arms.

18 She perceiveth that her merchandise is good: her candle goeth not out by night.

19 She layeth her hands to the spindle, and her hands hold the distaff.

20 She stretcheth out her hand to the poor; yea, she reacheth forth her hands to the needy.

21She is not afraid of the snow for her household: for all her household are clothed with scarlet.

22 She maketh herself coverings of tapestry; her clothing is silk and purple.

23 Her husband is known in the gates, when he sitteth among the elders of the land.

24 She maketh fine linen, and selleth it; and delivereth girdles unto the merchant.

25 Strength and honour are her clothing; and she shall rejoice in time to come.

26 She openeth her mouth with wisdom; and in her tongue is the law of kindness.

27 She looketh well to the ways of her household, and eateth not the bread of idleness.

28 Her children arise up, and call her blessed; her husband also, and he praiseth her.

29 Many daughters have done virtuously, but thou excellest them all.

30 Favour is deceitful, and beauty is vain: but a woman that feareth the LORD, she shall be praised.

31 Give her of the fruit of her hands; and let her own works praise her in the gates.

King James Version (KJV)

Blessings,

Candia Cumberbatch-Lucenius

Mama with my sisters and brothers after school-seems like yesterday!

Tribute to Our Mother Janet Magdaline Engene

Daddy

Missionary teachers she worked with in St. Lucia - from left to right: Sara Unger, Mary Cumberbatch (Mama), Bertha Tiessen, Ms. Klassen.

About the Author

I never considered myself a writer, but always had so many thoughts going on in my head, and wondered if I could possibly put them all down on paper.

Born on the Caribbean island of St. Lucia, along with my three sisters and two brothers, enjoyed the fun and poverty of living on an island. My parents made sure we all graduated from high school, so we would have the educational foundation needed to succeed. After graduating from high school, I decided to pursue a nursing career, because of always wanting to help take care of people; and even as a child had compassion on those suffering or in pain.

After graduating from Victoria Hospital School of

Nursing As a Registered Nurse – Midwife. My desire to educate and empower women goes way back when I developed a concern for the rapid increase in maternal and infant mortality, most of it due to teen pregnancies. In my role as a midwife in the hospital, in the community and public health, I was able to make a difference with education and counseling.

I relocated to Barbados, another Caribbean island, (which was my father's birthplace) for a number of years, where I continued my nursing career working in various areas of nursing. Two life changing events gave me a nudge to relocate again this time to the United States with my son and daughter. First was a short-lived marriage and subsequent divorce, and second the death of my father. I passed the U.S. State Board exam for nurses, continued working in various areas of nursing, and attended seminars, conferences and continuing education courses such as Legal Nurse Consultant with several certifications, one being a Certified Professional in Healthcare Management. A very rewarding experience was obtaining my Bachelors of Science in Nursing (BSN) and Masters of Science in Health Care

Administration.

About six years after my relocation to the U.S. I met a remarkable, handsome, intelligent young man, Jon S. Lucenius, who became my friend and about 2 years later – my husband. He made me laugh with his quirky, dry humor that most people didn't seem to get (but I did); he sent me roses for all or no occasion; he loved God and His Word; and learned to love my then teenage kids as his own (he has no biological children). We just celebrated our 20th anniversary, in 2016, and I'm still thankful to God for Jon's heart and life, his unwavering love and support for me, our kids and now grand-kids.

Getting closer to retirement, I made the decision to move out of bedside nursing; and have enjoyed working in Case Management, Utilization Review, Medical Records Review and Auditing for about 15 years, where I continue to enjoy the opportunity to work alongside other healthcare professionals to ensure continued care, as an advocate, educating people regarding managing their health and improving quality of life by taking control of their lives.

My continued quest to learn and understand the

accuracy of God's Word, led me to a non-denominational Christian bible fellowship, research and teaching ministry, where along with my husband we study and teach the Bible, so we can assist those interested in learning more about God, His Word, His will for our lives and how to practically incorporate those teachings into our daily lives. The goal is to manifest that "more than abundant life that the Word states Jesus Christ came to make available for us. John 10:10(b)" ... I (Jesus Christ), is come that they might have life and that they might have it more abundantly." In this role, as in many others during my life, I get to be a counselor, mediator, advocate, educator, communicator and change agent.

In 2009, I started a small women's group called 'Women of Virtue' (WOV) with a goal to bless, encourage, support, and empower as many women as I can. We have several women's events throughout the year – some planned, some spontaneous – for fun and fellowship, the highlights being our Annual Fall Women's Weekend Getaway followed soon after by our Christmas Party.

As I get older, I've been more focused on Natural Health and Healing endeavoring to help myself and as many as possible realize a better quality of life, by following the standards set forth in God's word. God made the body to heal itself and as we tap into that knowledge we can achieve improved health and healing naturally. As a nurse, my purpose is not to ignore conventional medicine, but to compliment it.

www.ingramcontent.com/pod-product-compliance
Lightning Source LLC
Chambersburg PA
CBHW060309050426
42448CB00009B/1774